THE WILL TO RESIST

also by j.d.tulloch

Undiscovered Paladins: Westward Rhymes Revisited
(39 West Press 2015)

Neutral Receding Lines: Road Rhymes, Volume Two
(39 West Press 2013)

Hypnotizing Lines: Road Rhymes, Volume One
(39 West Press 2011)

edited by j.d.tulloch

Desolate Country: We the Poets, United, Against Trump
(39 West Press 2017)

Prompts! A Spontaneous Anthology
(39 West Press 2016)

THE WILL TO RESIST
and psalms of anger, love & humanity

j.d.tulloch

39 WEST
PRESS

39 WEST PRESS
Kansas City, MO
www.39WestPress.com

Copyright © 2010 by j.d.tulloch

All rights reserved. No part of this book may be reproduced, scanned, or distributed in any printed or electronic form, including information storage and retrieval systems, without permission. Please do not participate in or encourage piracy of copyrighted materials in violation of the author's rights. Please purchase only authorized editions.

First Edition: December 2010

ISBN: 978-0-615-39361-2

Library of Congress Control Number: 2010910434

This book is a work of fiction. Names, characters, places, dates, and incidents are products of the author's imagination, or are used fictitiously, satirically, or as parody. Any resemblance to actual persons, living or dead, business establishments, events, or locales is entirely coincidental.

10 9 8 7 6 5 4 3 2

Design & Layout: j.d.tulloch

39WP-02A

"Today's youth culture is … constantly told that the only peace and happiness they can have will come to them through rugged individualism, through a focus on meeting self-centered needs … The will to resist can be tamed by a world that says everything can be as you want in the world of fantasy."

bell hooks
where we stand: class matters
(Routledge, 2000)

CONTENTS

psalms of anger

america	3
body bags	7
before ronald reagan	8
times square	12
thumb war	13
neon roses	14
gone	16
tomorrow	18
qt	19
sixteen acres	20
db	21

psalms of love

cry	25
goodbye	26
love	27
snowflakes	28
ecstasy	29
8 december 1980	30
my wish	32
seconds to years	33
the ocean	34
rosa	35

psalms of humanity
giant steps   39
addiction   40
agoraphobia   41
the fall   42
alone   43
exodus   47
pissing haiku   48
play   49
wicked haiku   51
murder in south central   52
mister entrepreneur   53
diamonds   55
fear   56
issues   58
five haiku   59

the will to resist   63

ps**alms of anger**

america

america—
land of the free

what happened to our democracy?

america—
land of the lost

freedom—
at what cost?

the quest for identity
from the images we see
god of america:
father tv

america incorporated—
absorbs our individuality
suppresses our creativity
rapes our virtue
quietly steals our souls
quietly takes our lives
quietly bankrupts our spirituality
while fueling the economy

the dow went up again
jobless claims at a five-week low
millionaires spawned by the thousand
the division of wealth continues to grow

but who gives a fuck about poverty?
and the housing projects of the negro city?
where a gunshot rings out
another dead child
another senseless loss

in the land where my fathers died
of thee i sing

let freedom ring
let freedom ring

freedom—
bought and sold like a cattle at auction
like a slave on the auction block
a past we can't escape
a past we won't embrace

freedom—
a social construction
a symbol of seduction
the warfare of civilization
the warfare of assimilation

america silently watches its eminent destruction

we can hegemonize the world
drop our bombs in the name of peace
but we can't feed the impoverished
dying on our city streets

social solution
social disillusion

build another prison
lock our black youth in jail
low income public housing
held without bail

shackles and chains
shackles and chains
break these shackles and gold chains

wait for your time
bide your time
do your time
do your time
for your crime
against humanity
against humility
against american sensibility

genocide
it's genocide
it's suicide

wait for your time
bide your time
bide your time
do your time

in america
home of the brave

america—
you don't know what we really crave

america—
home of the scared

freedom—
as if you ever cared

life (*indivisible*)
liberty (*injustice for all*)
the pursuit of happiness
it's the american pipe dream

but what happened to the dream of a king?

a gunshot rang out
another dead soul
another senseless loss

america died that day
the liberty bell did not ring

for martin luther king
of thee i sing

for martin luther king
let freedom ring

body bags

the body bags keep coming home
   but the caskets remain concealed
middle-east streets the combat zone
   roadside bombs line the battlefield

the body bags keep coming home
   no exit strategy prepared
our country's future placed on loan
   the fertile crescent scorched and seared

the body bags keep coming home
   no immediate end in sight
the seeds of terror firmly sewn
   by freedom's military might

the body bags keep coming home
   no army spouse should ever hear
that dreaded knock, the leading tone
   confirming a sacrosanct fear

the body bags keep coming home
   crusading tycoons the reason
no martyr could ever atone
   old glory's murderous treason

the body bags keep coming home
   let us shed a tear for the lost
till our souls have evolved and grown
   beyond warfare's damnable cost

before ronald reagan

before
ronald reagan
ronald mcdonald & monopoly
monopolies maintaining the media
the so-called *liberal* media
media whores
and crack whores

before
clarence thomas
tom cruise
tomahawk cruise missiles
tom greene
the green party
party balls
house party with kid n' play
new kids on the block
cabbage patch kids
the nicotine patch
patch adams the movie
adam sandler
adam curry's pod show
the man show
the cosby show
and "show me the money"

before
echo-boomers
gen net
generation me
generation X
ecstasy
X - E - K - G
and a plethora of other club drugs contained in a can of alphabet
  soup representing myriads of mind-altering madness

before
smurfette
safe sex
spandex pants
parachute pants
pink polos
pac-man
pokemon
ross perot
ross on *friends*
and shady friends on *seinfeld*

before
transformers
former interns
budget-cut international space stations
gas stations fixing prices
prices *fixing* iraq
iran contra
i ran so far away
"i don't recall"
don't ask don't tell
and tell-all talk shows creating a vicarious voyage of voyeurism

before
george dubya
the world wide web
the world wrestling federation
the world trade organization
the north american free trade agreement
free leonard peltier
free willie
slick willie
oil slicks in gulf of mexico
oil drilling in the alaskan wildlife refuge
and the alaskan valdez

before
acid rain
acid-washed jeans
stone-washed jeans
FUBU jeans
gene splicing
the gene map
the human genome project
the human right's campaign
the christian right
the christian coalition
the rainbow-push coalition
rainbow flags
PFLAG
the PTL
super PACs
soft money campaign contributions
and money driven suburbanites piloting SUVs while investing their futures in IRAs, CDs, mutual funds, 401Ks, tax shelters, and slippery stocks

before
MTV
"must see TV"
see all TV
reality TV
the real world
world news tonight
entertainment tonight
entertainment lawyers
lawyers on TV
court TV
mad TV
TV land
blockbusters on TV
"a blockbuster night"
nick at nite
a nightmare on elm street
and street gangs the Crips and the Bloods

before
contaminated blood
HIV
AIDS
farm aid
live aid
live net chat
chat room dates
date rape
born on dates
born in the USA
team USA
the dream team
and crumbling dreams tied up in dying dot coms

before
microsoft
microwaves
micro processing
word processing
"word to your mother"
welfare mothers
welfare reform
the Reform Party
tax reform
"no new taxes"
and tax *relief* for the bourgeois

before
bill gates
credit card bills
credit card debt
debit cards
and a nearly twenty trillion dollar national debt

before
ronald reagan …

times square

walking through midtown
november
two-thousand one
welcome to new york
it's
saturday night
        lights, pedestrians, action
my destination only blocks away
dinner
still on my mind
still digesting
somewhere in my small intestine
upset and overdressed
under the vegas-like excess littering
                    (illuminating)
the landscape of anger and tension
seeping from the sewers of manhattan while—
        a perfume of death permeates the ominous
        tone seducing a flock of tourists to
        times square
        to consume cheap collectibles—
families follow the aroma of
freshly baked bread prepared by
grandmother on thanksgiving day

thumb war

one two three four
i declare a thumb war

on ...
crooks in the Capitol
capital punishment
punishing potheads
head in the Oval Office
office cubicles
Broadway musicals
music award shows
shows on the TBN
invading sovereign nations
nationalism
unbridled patriotism
the Patriot Act
acts of terror
terrorism committed by US
U.S. foreign policy
policy-ing the world
the World Bank
world hunger
Hungry Man dinners
dinner around the television
TV culture
and a culture that declares war on crime
                                      Christmas
                                      Islam
                                      illiteracy
                                      Iraq
                                      Afghanistan
                                      drugs and obesity

one two three four
i declare a thumb war

neon roses

   stone suburban parapets proficiently protect
     imprisoned municipal migrants beneath
       snow littered

   mountain peaks of desert heat in sterile stucco shelters
     whose only variant the color of trim surrounding
       second floor

   windows of time quickly commuting fifteen
     miles or forty-five minutes eastbound down
       charleston metamorphosing

   martin luther king appropriating i-15 to paradise: the
     fabulous las vegas strip shows and gaming floors—
       cha ching—

   of faux metropolises magically mimicking cultured cities
     stemming with taciturn tourists touting the authentic
       replica arc

   de triumphant eiffel tower of babbling bellagio
     fountains flowing freely from lake mead to new york
       harbor's lady

   liberty through venetian canals and valleys of king tut's tomb
     deeply dug deficits dooming dealers of draw poker to a
       luxorious life

   of fleecing frustrated family men and women
     dancing dangerously close to naked extinction
       surviving solely

   on the static sounds of a hapless hope fed by the
     unquenchable appetites of stingy slot machines and
       russian roulette

wheels spinning chambered webs of a vanquished
  doom blooming fully beneath a bounty of
    neon roses

revealing unconquerable odds hungrily harvested
  by rows of craps tables irrigated with plastic
    cow chips

whose intrinsic value seemingly reflects vibrantly
  useless monopoly money flippantly flung like a pair of
    dice drenched

with the last drop of blood forfeited by
  the fatted calf of greedy gamblers to
    callous casinos

gone

In the Internet café,
hipsters come and go,
surfing wirelessly,
effortlessly adoring
their pieces, their Galaxies, their Motos.

Three screennames from which to choose,
three identities to assume.

He says, "I'll have a café mocha, Grande.
Four shots, not three ... if there is room."

The chat room seems a little fin today,
but Hipster A
needs to vent some rage,
needs to update his Twitter feed or Facebook page,
needs to post another page,
another post-modern blog by a nihilist sage,
exposing his life story for voyeurs to ingest,
kitsch for all to see
in the shallow sea
of DARPA technology,
sipping his coffee,
creating his own paparazzi,
photographs and selfies frozen in finality:
the eco-boomer's therapy,
the Google Generation's reality.

Gone.

The barista busses the vacant table,
preparing the space for another deck cronkite,
a paranoid prophet whose cowlicks and unshaven face
face the world with an i-Phone in one hand,
peeling an orange with the other.

"Brother," says Hipster B.
"Can you spare some change?
I need some kale for another Café au lait.
Frank Einstein died today,"
I heard Madman say
while running away
from another day
of truth, light, and the American way.

In the Internet café,
hipsters come and go,
surfing aimlessly,
effortlessly adoring another shot of espresso.

Enter Hipster C:
"I'll move to Williamsburg someday.
Brooklyn that is ...
The North Side ...
Close to the L-Train."

Tragically unaware of the gentrification
and rising rents of this former bohemian domain,
platinum carrying scenesters
dominate this demographic of seduction
by high-rise construction
and waterfront rezoning
in the latest incarnation
of the SoHo-Effect of Manhattanization.

Artists flee to Philly,
which is the sixth borough we now know;
while in the Internet café,
hipsters come and go.

tomorrow

The day before yesterday,
  a friend told me he wanted to move to Brooklyn,
Williamsburg to be specific.

Yesterday,
  I wrote a poem vis-à-vis the Williamsburg hipsters,
of whom I'm a sarcastic, cynical critic.

Today,
  I met a phlebotomist whose boyfriend, manfriend,
is some sort of Williamsburg artist, how pathetic.

Tomorrow,
  I'll advise another chum, birth another verse,
and descry another bloodletter, how terrific.

qt

Dear Sir or Madam [Unread Internet Contact Form Inbox],

After phoning local law enforcement officials, your well-trained front counter employee [dropout] chose not to sell me specific grocery items [whiskey] in my gallant endeavor [enabling attempt] to supply sustenance [hope] for two downtrodden gentlemen [vagrants] catching a breather [loitering] on the sidewalk in front of your store. Apparently, QT is only a "safe place" for people who have arrived in motorized vehicles and have bathed within the last week [or so]. I will no longer patronize this establishment for my gasoline and convenience store needs [cigarettes & blunt shells] as a result of this blatant and unjustifiable discrimination of two tax paying [homeless] Vietnam vets [heroes] who happen to transcend the mainstream norm of socialized consumer [soccer mom] by choosing not to become appendages [sheep] of mega-corporate, megalomaniacal madness [America].

Thank you [go fuck yourself].

sixteen acres

sixteen acres in Lower Manhattan
twin monuments of man's engineering might
twin towers defending the city's right

sixteen acres in Lower Manhattan
twin targets of the radical jihadist fight
twin soldiers falling into oblivion's night

sixteen acres in Lower Manhattan
prime real estate in the financial center
battlefield graveyard, near nuclear winter

2800 screaming voices in Lower Manhattan
casualties of American imperialism
fatalities of American materialism

2800 screaming voices in Lower Manhattan
martyrs of national patriotism
commodities of national symbolism

hear their cries/wipe the tears from their eyes
as we sing the jingoist anthems of the past
as we fill our cars with Middle East gas

pray for the oil
pay for the oil
remember the attacks on American soil

where two-fifths of forty acres and a mule
plus three-fifths a person
equals a whole in the Big Apple

db

    green—
garbage dumpsters; tourists on the corner of the third street promenade.

    manna—
from heaven; spoon fed by the hand of god.

    domicile—
subconscious visions; apparitions of an undiscovered country spawn surreal illusions dancing around the cemetery.

    carolyn—
a seizure; another DB; supplementary DB without opportunity.

forensic unit—
    uncomfortable tension; the loss of gravity surrounds eager expectations wallowing in misery.

    shaking—
a cigarette; yellow tape circling the alley; red lights flashing; flashing fortuitous allusions as perceptions of reality ignore intimate intentions ricocheting under the brevity.

    life—
capital; cuisine; apparel; asylum; a warm place to sleep.

    time—
existing; expired; immutable sleep.

    death—
malicious misconceptions of a befuddled mystery pander to pathetic rationalizations floating around insanity.

       reminiscence of atrocity—
formidable frustrations of a vanquished humanity transcend
ambiguous aggravations emancipating captivity.

       carolyn—
another exiled individual; another from the streets; one more DB;
one more conquered american pipe dream; DOA on the corner
of the third street promenade; just another DB.

       why god?

psalms of love

cry

i'm not afraid to cry;
it's sad when people go away.

jesus wept one day,
but i cannot remember why …

                    oh yeah,
                    now i recall …

                    he arrived too late
                    to save his friend

goodbye

she sits solitarily
  studying anatomy
  sipping green tea
  silently knitting a sweater

her tousled hair
  angelic eyes
  sensual smile
    tempts me
    cheers me
    guides me
        like a lighthouse
        leading lost wayfarers
        seeking
          solace
        seeking
          shelter
        seeking
       someone, something
special

she glances at me again
  peers inquisitively
  penetrates my mind
  palpitates my heart

she stands to leave
  stops by my table
  slowly raises her hand, waves
  softly smiles, says

goodbye

love

    some say love is dead/some say love is a self-righteous myth masquerading as something it is not/some say love clouds and obscures our better judgements

    sometimes in our daily lives we become so caught up in ourselves/selfishness/the triviality of insignificant things/the pursuit to achieve a sense of happiness/acceptance that we fail to notice/perceive the aesthetic beauty in our world and the transcendent beauty deep within each other

    we unsuitably define ourselves and try to find contentment/delight/ecstasy through thoughtlessness/vanity/fucking/materialism/modern capitalism/industrialization/urbanization/commercialization

    mass culture constructs ideologies in conflict with the notions of what actually should be important in our lives

    selfish greed/inherent insecurities/the quest for identity within a society of rampant avariciousness conceals visceral feelings of equality and love

    this indoctrination/brainwashed mentality/propaganda presented by the puppet master pulling our strings/social conditioning/selling of our souls for the ephemeral narcissism of earthly pleasures/hubris reaches deep

    the inculpable child playing with her dolls under the pulchritude of the blue sky becomes perverted by the folly of humanity

    tainted by futility we acquiesce to the servitude associated with becoming appurtenances of civilization

    we are not free/we are vassals of assimilation/we are a vacuous people destitute of a veritable hope, a hope that ameliorates humankind and not just the individual

    unless we find love/resurrect love/live love we will become carrion man decaying on the earth's surface while the temporal structures of avarice/frivolity/futility/devastation remain

snowflakes

snowflakes
remind me of
the time in sixth
grade when
dad and i
built a snowman
in the front yard only
to see it melt away like
the dreams of one's youth
slowing evaporating under the
intensity of the cold sun until
nothing remains but a
teardrop

ecstasy

peak around the corner
only a matter of time

sights
sounds

touchdown
stimuli of the mind

hail a comet in wrigleyville
traveling towards the magnificent mile

floating on overloaddrive
rolling down chicago's nile ...

>   supernova stars surround sirens screaming soft
>   against horns honking harmoniously aloft
>   a rabid rocket reaching a black heavenly hole
>   hiding happy hush-hush ecstatic enigmas stole
>   somewhere downtown the sears tower stands
>   scraping the skyline leaving lunar lands
>   lurking luxuriously near notions of
>   nighttime travels tumbling towards lost love ...

down in the gutter
the comet loses its tail

jump towards the curb
and wait to set sail

thoughts reverberate
sacred stimuli of the mind

peak around the corner
only a matter of time

8 december 1980

all my life's been a long slow knife
somebody please
please help me
get me out of this hell
i'm drowning in the sea of hatred
i'm lying in the darkness
i can't get to sleep
i don't know what to do
all i want is the truth

you know life can be long
one day at a time is all we do
i don't wanna die
it's getting better all the time
you know that it's a lie
i can't get it through my head
trying to change the whole wide world
you don't have to worry in heaven or hell
you got to feel something

trust me darlin'
everything is clear in my heart
we're deep in each other's hearts
love will turn you on
love has opened my eyes
love is a flower you got to let it grow
love is wanting, asking, needing to be loved
i promise you anything

come on listen to me, come on listen to me

"an unspeakable tragedy"
spoke howard cosell
on 8 december 1980

*"john lennon
outside of his apartment building
on the west side of new york city
shot twice in the back
rushed to roosevelt hospital
dead on arrival"*

remember, remember today
was it just a dream?
i found out
who am i?
nobody knows but me
what can I say?
the dream is over
i got to tell you goodbye
i'm sorry that i made you cry

hold on john, john hold on

let's walk over rainbows like leprechauns
singin, "power to the people today"

we are all water from different rivers
if you don't believe me take a look
that's why it's so easy to meet
we are all water in this vast, vast ocean

someday you'll join us
someday we'll evaporate together

and the world will be as one

Note: The preceding poem, a *cento*, is composed of lines lifted from songs written by John Lennon.

my wish

my christmas wish list
depicts an unmaterialistic gift

lost in the consumeristic
excess of holiday rhetoric

outside the fabric
of shopping mall madness

i simply ask for only this:
a loving christmas day kiss

seconds to years

drunken revelers euphorically assemble into a crowded pub that
resembles a high school house party

        pay a ten dollar cover
        (for a champagne toast)

        grab the nearest warm bodied stranger
        (and steal a smoky kiss)

        celebrate the dawning of another year
        (of forgotten resolutions)

as their parents sit at home alone
with each other and ~~dick clark~~ ryan seacrest

        count down the seconds
        (for a champagne toast)

        share a sacred kiss with the one
        (they've chosen not to forget)

        celebrate the dawning of another year
        (of unrealized dreams)

        and the financial hardships
        (of a partnership)

        that at some point devolved into Hayes code cinema
        (with separate beds and silent sexual desires)

surviving solely on the familiarity of an old love that
values companionship over the cosmic loneliness of ladies night

the ocean

waves crash into the shore
(with power unsurpassed).

high tides! low tides! riptides! a jetty!
swells that reach far and vast.

friends come and enemies go,
turn their backs on spiritual serenity,

yet unconditionally it gives,
freely gives of all its energy:

a love that is there for the taking,
a precious gift for all to share,

rhymes of ancient mariners
resolutely ring, sing cries from the deep,

"i am the ocean,
reach out to me if you dare."

i *am* the ocean,
reach out to *me* if you dare.

rosa

rosa parks,
the last american heroine,

interred in a detroit cemetery
and presented

a first class bus ticket
to heaven

psalms of humanity

giant steps

he wanders into the wine bar
audaciously orders a martini dry
sounds the jazz trio's giant steps
reverberating off the tin ceiling

fans ruffling his benny hinn comb-over
coxcomb's not the typical barfly
on the wall street journal captured
under his arm wheeling and dealing

cell phone clipped to his kuiper belt
like captain kirk's communicator
velcroed to his khaki dockers and
lieutenant uhura's bluetooth headset

protruding from his miracle ear
muff diving sugar daddy suitor
who wins at last thanks not
to his charm but his red corvette

addiction

couch-ridden suburban junkies shoot oxy, mainline morphine, fix themselves to the temporary tempo of a slowed drum circle, a retarded circadian rhythm, a government-sanctioned pharmaceutical coma in the depressing drug-den living room of a low end provider, dealer, server of life's hope, while tweakers wait anxiously, impatiently, for their next fixes of ice, go fast, crystal meth, chasing the white dragon, ready to sell their last earthly possession (or their best friend's), choosing alertness and insomnia over the mundane madness of McDonald's Happy Meals and an internal happiness inherently found in dead-end corporate employment and inexpensively produced reality shows that distract us from the importance of family and friends, only reminded of friends and family by a cell phone commercial that encourages us to stay in touch, reach out and touch someone on the information super-highway, trafficking millions and millions of terabytes around the terra-firma, translucent towers transferring texts in lieu of interpersonal communication, Facebook, Twitter, and WhatsApp messages, walls & buzzes in 140 characters, creating a pseudo-reality, a quasi-gospel, falsely projecting to others what we wish our lives were like, attempting to capture fame to fifteen followers for internet eternity in a society that has created a social-circle of narcissistic neophytes who piously attempt, by following a fraudulent fad, to find a place in a post-modern world that says we can all have what we want by making minimum monthly payments, creating insurmountable deficits to be paid by future generations for the benefit of instant profits and selfish shareholder greed.

what happened to the will to resist?

the American ~~condition~~ addiction.

agoraphobia

i never pay attention
to the weatherman

but he ruined my day
when i heard him say

with conviction and sleight of hand
that it would be sunny and fifty

(but it never reached thirty)
so i didn't leave the house

the fall

```
gone to get a milkshake
or a mandrake
root beer float
```

said the note
neatly typed
on stryped

stationery
nary
seen

between
camus' *la chute*
and my wet suit

alone

I wake up every morning, the eastern sun shining through the dusty blinds of my bedroom window, and ask myself what we have done to deserve this fate.

I stagger from the tattered sheets of my bed, alone, and make my way into a shower of warm water, attempting to briefly resuscitate my psyche for another day of nothingness.

I stand in the shower, and the water penetrates my flesh and soothes my inner essence, momentarily taking me to a place on another plane, another dimension, extremely far from where I currently exist.

I see a flowing river of serenity, unpolluted by industrialization, winding its way between a sea of gorgeous green trees, blanketing the countryside as far as the eye can see.

I see brilliant blue skies, a blue like no other I have seen before, and sparse snow white clouds caress softly along the horizon, reflecting themselves back down to the river below.

I see a radiant red sun, the same sun that peers through my window every morning, but it is different, and yet it is the same, still providing life to all things it watches over.

I see one mystical mountain, alone, protruding from the fertile earth as the river runs mysteriously up this giant mass of granite, disappearing in a cloud of mist hovering around the mountaintop.

I see or hear no signs of animal life, only the vast vegetation and the simple sounds of a light breeze blowing through the trees, rustling the lingering leaves against each other.

I stand watching in amazement, breathing in the vigor of the environment, and as I start to explore, suddenly, I find myself back in the shower, shivering, as the once warm water has turned bitterly cold.

I have involuntarily returned to my reality after temporarily transcending the time and place we perceive as the present, yet still longing for a permanent escape to a simpler place, free of all frivolity, vanity, and greed.

I, however, am a hypocrite, but my hypocrisy goes only so far as my steel internal-combustion machine with molded rubber wheels carries me along man-made asphalt paths to my destination.

I stop for a moment, taking in the visual vastness of the city and the aesthetic alchemy associated with the happy hectic pace of the slaves to the routine, incoherent of their dire need for emancipation.

I see no serenity, only insanity, as pollution and waste in every form stain the once unencumbered euphoria of the firmament and the once untrodden space of the realm below.

I see many mountains, or rather molded monuments of iron and glass, disappearing in clouds of low lying smog as they reach upward for the heavens, apparently grasping for the hand of god.

I see thousands of people aimlessly wandering the streets, alone, scurrying from one bountiful building to the next, oblivious to the truth, guided falsely by the spoon-fed propaganda of the political polemicists.

I see through this river of deceit, its mechanisms of manipulating the masses, and how it subtly brainwashes and influences our thoughts through the misrepresentation of apparent trustworthy vices that merely masquerade as something they are not.

I see lost souls searching for happiness through the only means they know as expectations of success, achievement, and desire become nothing more than conditioned responses to a falsely placed stimulus, a misguided madness of melancholy.

I see pompous politicians legislating morality—using rhetoric that spews from their mouths like the venom from a snake's fangs—and reaping circles of *success* by pandering to over-zealous Jesuits, thereby coyly advancing their own corrupt and self-righteous directives.

I see a once neoteric nation that offered an escape from the tempest of tyranny, the legislative power and control of the church, now realigning itself with the judgmental maxims of hate that hide behind the façade of organized religion, the most controlling and influencing political party in the history of humankind.

I see the judgmental, vile contempt and utter ungodly hatred that these self-proclaimed Christians have for those who are unlike themselves, directly contradicting the second (and most important) commandment of their leader and savior: "Love one another."

I see how they misrepresent and misinterpret the peaceful words of a man who taught tolerance and equality, love and loyalty, faith and hope, and use his words to selectively condemn *anarchists* like me who have broken their mirror of reality and explored uncharted ground on the other side.

I have eaten from The Forbidden Tree, much like Adam and Eve, and my blindness, or rather tunnel vision, has been expanded to another dimension, a dimension capable of perceiving and comprehending shapes, colors, words, images, and signs that before were only as visible as the dimmest and faintest star in the infinite night sky.

I am their worst nightmare, the eastern sun promoting peace and sanctity into the minds of the unenlightened while simultaneously extinguishing an already waning belief sewn in an investment that will never reap the harmony and spiritual accord it has promised.

exodus

if i made a billion bucks
delivering women to the

promised land by pledging
an unconditional covenant

to commercial conglomerates,
would i procure a fifty million

dollar golden calf for myself
atop mount sinai, secluding

me from the habitat for humanity
homes humbly hidden beneath

the dead sea of the ninth ward?
i hope not …

pissing haiku

bigot donald trump
  pisses his adult diaper
while praising himself

        bin laden pisses
          the bottom of the sea while
        admiring allah

                the white house pisses
                  on the constitution when
                spying on dissent

        king kong pisses
          himself, stinks of shit, and still
        attracts the blonde babe

jesus christ pisses
  standing up like every
man living or dead

play

the thundering roar of crowded voices
reflects the inanity of the passing humility

docile drones espouse selfish, masculine maxims
(second hand smoke filtered by TV morality)

post-modern hipster
neo-hipster

faux-hipster
emo-hipster

new-wave vegan hipster
frat-jock hipster

suburban hipster
hippie hipster:

trustafarian

commodities of a self-centered culture whose only solace
spawns from the repetitive drums of generation *indie*

cradled by the latent hand of streaming media
they consume conspicuously consume

cravedesirewant
the drumbeat sets them free

trappedcagedenslavedconfined
wild animals held captive in the city of commercial civilization

participants of amorous apathy
products of economic slavery

pianissimo …

synchronous sounds shape shivering silhouettes
mistaking madness in lieu of social sanity

fortissimo …

the latent hand molds the clay
covertly performing a sweeping lobotomy

the latent hand molds the clay
transforming the malleable mass into a void less clone

lacking individuality
possessing popularity

manufacturing materiality
securing superficiality

cradled by the manifest hand of indie media
they consume conspicuously consume

cravedesirewant
trappedcagedenslavedconfined

they play
 (we play)

press play
press the repeat button intuitively

the drumbeat sets them free
the drumbeat sets us   free

wicked haiku

the wicked white witch
  slyly seduces its prey
with alluring s(p/m)ells

the wicked white witch
  cleverly controls its prey
with sparkling s(c/h)am smiles

the wicked white witch
  tenderly fucks its prey with
masterful mind games

the wicked white witch
  decapitates its prey with
deafening silence

murder in south central

Moses—
  killed an Egyptian man
  refused to circumcise his son

  Then, a burning bush spoke to him ...
    he delivered the enslaved from bondage
    led his people down a path of righteousness
      was denied entry into the promised land
      was put down by his vengeful god

Tookie—
  allegedly killed four
  refused to admit his guilt

  Then, the voice of reason spoke to him ...
    he delivered the enslaved from bondage
    led his followers from a path of crime
      was denied life without parole
      was executed by a vengeful governor

Moral—
  don't trust in gods or governors to do the right thing

mister entrepreneur

mister entrepreneur
plays his devious game in a world he created
      with his father's funds
      with the lives of those he employs
average people
(with average dreams)
trying their best
      to make their way
      to earn their pay
trying their best
      to support their families
      to avoid the calamities
            of his living chess game
            of self-indulgent fantasy
            of sardonic strategy
manipulated solely for the sheer drama
            of power
            of entertainment
by mister entrepreneur
in a self-righteous quest
(a narcissist's best attempt)
      to prove
      to establish
that the universe in fact does revolve around
      his every act
      his every move
            of unrelentless firings
            of unmerciless screamings
            of throwing temper tantrums
like a tiny toddler
(an overgrown infant)
when mister entrepreneur
does not
      get his way
      get what he wants pleases desires

mister entrepreneur sleeps alone tonight
(and every night)
since money cannot
purchase buy persuade
someone to love him and his devious ways

mister entrepreneur
        sleep well
                tonight

diamonds

Branded by his mom with the name Useless,
   A man lived forlorn, struggling to subsist.

Deceit and larceny for him the norm.
   Broken promises, his one true art form.

He was scarred and scared from childhood abuse,
   Depressed and alone, ensnared in a noose.

Squandering each day upon his deathbed,
   From duty and blame, he constantly fled.

Despite hefty dreams and charms of voodoo,
   Exploiting catspaws was all that he knew.

Fresh prey angled after battered gulls spent,
   Easily discarded without consent.

He owned no guilt, just a hole in his heart
   (A gaping lesion that kept him apart

From acknowledging love and living life
   Without vexing allies and forging strife).

With no truth to tell, virtue to extol,
   He drowned deep inside his selfish fishbowl.

But one mark loved him despite what he stole;
   That chump saw diamonds, not coal for a soul.

fear

as i flip through the broadcast channels past peter jacksons king kong stopping on the trinity broadcasting network where two devout christians try to persuade unsaved viewers to choose narnia as an angelic alternative to the satanically influenced harry potter films claiming god covertly weaved his gospel throughout the narrative while praising disney for daring to evangelize through secular media as strict southern baptists boycott the same company for providing benefits to same sex partners of their employees when kirk cameron growing pains mike seaver comes on telling sinners they will spend all of eternity swimming in a sea of fire unless they believe jesus expired on a cross to save them from their senses while judging people for their own personal belief systems when his personal savior said judge not and be not judged because maybe society pinned king kong to the empire state building to pay the price for our imperfections or tacked ronald mcdonald to the golden arches as penance for the transgressions of enlightened evangelicals who cant let individuals be who they are without trying to convert them over to their parochial philosophy using machiavellian methods of submission obedience and fear when HIV positive magic johnson appears marketing the new lincoln mark LT pickup truck to african american males apparently attempting to lower the target demographic from sixty to "nigga" as COPS cuff and arrest a well-dressed man of color robbing a late-night liquor store with a sharp stiletto in his hand while fleeing the scene in his large lincoln navigator because the nightly news says knives are as dangerous as any gun wielding sunni radical cleric whom iraqi courts disqualified from the historic elections since he allegedly had ties to sadams baath party of genocide when a retired army colonel efficiently trained at reading the teleprompter responds to the buxom blonde broadcasters question by confidently claiming that voting is crucial in assimilating all liberated iraqis into democratic politics instead of terror and violence as another national network nefariously names the fearless iraqi people person of the year for spilling

purple ink on their free fingers instead of the innocent blood
of american troops who daily defend the freedom of all voting
age american citizens to engage in exciting elections every four
years where the courageous leader of our country is sometimes
(s)elected by activist judges who favor states rights over federal
power and support the constitutional rights of pregnant women
and horny gay men to choose what they will do with their own
bodies including shoving big macs down their throats and
fucking condomlessly while worshipping a hot blonde virgin
who will not requite the undying love of a colossal hairy ape

issues

her name was erin
but ron thought she said "error"
(a mistake)

but his friend phil o. sophy
rescorrected his blunder
and pined about the free will of god

until zarathurstra spake
to jean-babtiste clemance
and superman fell from the sky

five haiku

1
time's certain curse
   fades in relativity's
future cessation

2
truth absolute
   flips over a coin to for
see the other side

3
salvation from
   society's secular
slavery: solitude

4
the earth's beauty
   eludes those who wallow in
the mire of greed

5
be passersby by
   bypassing the freeway to
financial freedom

the will to resist

I've watched the best minds of our generation erode away
into silken linens of infomercials and soda pop ads as
megacorporations manufacture consent for the bewildered herd
who have yet to escape Plato's cave.

Jesus' grave. i believe he rolled over again. Or wait. Did someone
roll away the stone from the entrance to his tomb?

The womb. How fast nine months flies. Then you're sixty-four,
sixty grand in debt, and waiting for one more Valentine before
the Social Security checks arrive in the mail: eight-hundred
forty-two dollars of pure, government-subsidized fun.

Helios (or was it Apollo) passed by again: his golden chariot
consistently pulling the sun around our habitat for the six
billionth successive solar cycle. You'd think he'd be tired by now.
Too bad Zeus won't let him retire.

You're fired: Trump or monkey hair? The strength of Sampson
beamed via satellite into the living rooms of millions and
projected via RGB, LCD onto the alter of worship that shapes and
molds our very existence. Pray to the Nielsen god who so humbly
serves its media-giant masters: the whores of Babylon ruled by
the universal pimp of advertising revenue.

What to do. The traffic light signals go. Incandescent green
guides us from street corner to street corner as we busily hustle
to nowhere in an incessant quest of repetition from one day to
the next.

Convenience. The convenience store. The gathering place.
The temple of life from which we fuel our vehicles, purchase
powerball phantasies, and munch on microwaved burritos and
crusty corndogs so generously made available to us by the kind
folks at Sysco.

Disco and Techno. Pop and Soul. Rock 'n' Roll. Hip-hop and
bebop. And R & B. The stylus (the laser) follows the grooves from

beginning to end and back again while anxious teens relax to the beat of the drums, consume the rhythm of the bass, and dissent against the mediocrity of ma and pa.

Shock and awe. A tsunami of rockets and missiles barrage a helpless and unknowing people who adore a god not so dissimilar from our own. Where is the cult of celebrity when it comes to raising relief for the displaced and innocent inhabitants of Iraq?

Crack is whack. Ice to be precise. Twisted lies and damaged lives. Not the lives of those addicted to a quick fix, a first time high that in no way will ever be equaled again, but rather the ruins of rubble left behind deep within the souls of those selfless enablers who only do what is humanely possible in order to triumph over an evil enemy in an unwinnable war whose obtuse obsession makes sociopaths out of social beings.

To be or not to be. Hamlet's dilemma. To cease or to expire. To wither into desire. To lurch into the mire and smolder in a cauldron of fire. Shadrach, Meshach, and Abednego. Phlegyas guiding lost souls across the river Styx. Sartre conferring being onto Being: luminosity.

Generosity. Transcending the self. Translating freedom. Existing as a beacon unto humanity. Lighting the route for wayward travelers. The sirens guiding Jason. The shoreline is approaching. Wait Sisyphus. That bolder must be heavy. Why do you push it up that hill at such a regular interval only to let it roll back down upon you?

Enkidu. Lifeless Enkidu. Gilgamesh's noble quest for immortality. The fountain of life. The bread of being. This is my body which i shed for unconditional love. Hal and Falstaff. Francesca and Paulo. Othello and Desdemona. David and Jonathan. Jesus and Judas. How easily we fail. How unabashedly frail. How feeble our psyches. Utnapishtim. Show us thy way. Build us an ark. Can Noah come out and play?

Not today Vladimir. Let's wait until tomorrow Estragon. Godot will surely appear to us then. He showed himself to Moses, to Hammurabi, and asked Abraham to sacrifice his only son. Patience. We must have patience. Godot moves in mysterious ways. He's not coming. Nietzsche killed him. But whom did Mohammad see? Siddhartha definitely spotted him at the 7-11 eating chimichangas with Elvis and Santa.

Satan. Milton's Satan snorted with satisfaction the day Jesus commended his spirit unto the father, or was it his virgin mother? The day Eve provided Adam with the fruit from the forbidden tree. Eve was a virgin too, then. The day humanity gained the knowledge of good and evil. Oh, our virgin minds. We were naked but now we are clothed. We were blind but now we see. But what do we see? Truth and beauty? Good and evil? Right and wrong? God and mammon? No. Janet Jackson's breast. Somebody get a fig leaf.

If you have ears, you should hear. But what should you hear? Hear ye, here ye. Unto thee, proclaimed Jamie Foxx, a new savior has arisen in the District of Columbia, in the city of Washington, which is Obama, our lord. Better than another virgin Bush bearing barren gifts of frankincense and myrrh, oil and coal, black gold, if that is your goal. If that is your crusade. Another point for the home team. Another point for the American Dream. The fans in the stands scream. The fans in the stands dream.

Dream. Dream of a kingdom that is here at hand. Imagine that you have only one chance to comprehend a reality that is not of this world. Imagine that you have only one chance to transcend a reality that is not of this world. Nirvana. Swarga. Paradise. Mag Mell. Valhalla. Heaven. The kingdom is here at hand. If you seek, you will find, and if you knock, it will be opened unto you.

Camus. Albert Camus. The judge penitent sees the stranger and identifies with the slave who revolts against the master and is thereby reborn into an essence that proceeds existence in the same way an adult becomes like a child and is born again, subsequently dismissing the dogma and socialization of the Roman Empire, American hegemony, Fundamentalist Christianity, and a capitalist consumer corporate culture that falsely projects delusions of reality onto billboard marquees in the name of Lord God Almighty American Dollar.

Holler. Holler. Holler. The cock crows thrice. Three strikes and you're out. Abide these three: faith, hope, and love. These three bear witness: the father, the word, and the holy spirit. The trinity: ABC, NBC, and CBS. Catch the FOX that spoils the vines and sours the tender grapes setting the children's teeth on edge. Know them by the fruits they bare. Know them by the lambskin they wear.

Dare to care. Care to dare a society that believes beauty is youth and youth is a lifelong customer with an infinite credit line and a pre-required desire only to find contentment and credence in material merchandise produced by serf labor in Third World countries that lack the weapons of mass destruction to defend themselves against American imperialism, or as Dubya Christ so eloquently proclaimed it: the aggressive expansion of freedom.

Another kingdom. A kingdom of cornucopia and self-loathing. A kingdom of this world. Ask yourself one question: how is an individual free when Tomahawk cruise missiles and Apache attack helicopters (please note the irony in the naming conventions the Pentagon uses for its WMDs) impose a semantic emancipation, a fictitious freedom, a deceitful democracy, an illusory liberty in the guise of a fascist, free-enterprise, state-subsidized, propagandized plutocratic-oilgarchy?

Malarkey. Absurd gibberish. Bunk drivel. Nonsensical idiocy. Poppycock. Senseless silliness. Inane madness. Insane folly. Psychotic lunacy. Mindless sanity brought to you by the kind folks at Merck and Pfizer, where your health insurance dollar finances the Congressionalized, legalized drug trade that medicates millions of malcontent suburbanites mistakenly missing the message of Marx while solely relying on the machinations of misunderstood self-help manuscripts and mass-marketed miracle remedies.

Maladies. Difficulties. Complex intricacies. Minutiae. May cause drowsiness, headaches, stomach cramps, anal bleeding, rapid heart rate, pre-mature ejaculation, and rickets. Consult your physician, pharmacist, psychic, pastor, priest, proctologist, periodontist and/or podiatrist if symptoms persist for more than ten working days. Do not take if pregnant, nursing, lactating, fornicating, teething, sleeping, drinking, eating, smoking, living, and/or breathing without first conferring with your psychiatrist, psychologist, pathologist, pediatrician, personal trainer, pizza delivery guy, phone sex operator, and the pope.

Pope Benedict the sixteenth. Bye bye Prada Pope. Bye bye Vicar of Gucci. Bye bye His Holy Queenness. Praise this pompous priest's predilection for donning designer duds and pathetically promoting pedophilia and pederasty by banning celibate queers from the seminary. Maybe the new pontiff's portrait will look just as fabulous on the face of the Vatican's euro coins? Render unto God what is Caesar's! What is St. Peter's? Denial. I know not the man who ran the moneychangers from the temple. Didn't FDR promise to run them from the Capitol?

Das Kapital. The wealth of nations. The wealth of American citizens confiscated by the IRS, laundered by Congress, and supplied as subsidy by the Pentagon to national *defense* contractors. Didn't Eisenhower prophesize the military-industrial-congressional complex's unwarranted influence endangered our liberties and democracy? Take heed: our eternal war economy profits corporate carpetbaggers by bombarding dissenting autonomous nations back to the middle east ages while the drowning residents of New Orleans suffer shell-shock, slowly sinking in a shit-swamp of Uncle Sam's synecdochic stew.

Whew. Whose balls are blue? Tired televangelists, tempted by happy hookers sucking the holy sacrament, tout the second-coming, succumbing spiritually to an amorous apocalyptical climax centered selfishly around soulless-satisfaction. See the slithering serpent slyly seduce, sentencing sinners to damnation save you send your savings soon. Act now. Do not delay. For salvation you must pay the price for your shortcomings. A vicarious execution and premature resurrection your only penance.

Ring the bell. Sink in your hooks. Seek permanent peace and holistic happiness through selfish individualism, through a fixated focus on satisfying self-centered needs. Seek slavery. Seek subjugation. Tame and domesticate your will to resist a world that teaches desire can be reality—a castle in the sky, an effete El Dorado, a useless Utopia—by chasing, capturing, presently possessing everything possible as if your spiritual survival singularly subsisted on sadly serving a corrupt civilization of narcissistic need and egocentric fantasy. Or … transcend your self and seek a selfless love that saves us all.

j.d.tulloch is a writer, filmmaker, and social activist. He is the founder of 39 West Press and has worked in broadcast radio and for the management team of the late Godfather of Soul, James Brown.